PROSE POEMS

THE BOOKS OF

KAHLIL GIBRAN

"His power came from some great reservoir of spiritual life, else it could not have been so universal and so potent, but the majesty and beauty of the language with which he clothed it were all his own."

CLAUDE BRAGDON

The Madman · 1918
Twenty Drawings · 1919
The Forerunner · 1920
The Prophet · 1923
Sand and Foam · 1927
Jesus, the Son of Man · 1928
The Earth Gods · 1931
The Wanderer · 1932
The Garden of the Prophet · 1933
Prose Poems · 1934
Nymphs of the Valley · 1948
Spirits Rebellious · 1949
A Tear and a Smile · 1950
The Broken Wings · 1959
The Voice of the Master · 1960
A Self-Portrait · 1960
Thoughts and Meditations · 1961
Spiritual Sayings · 1963

PROSE POEMS

by

Kahlil Gibran

Translated from the Arabic by

Andrew Ghareeb

With a Foreword by

Barbara Young

HEINEMANN : LONDON

William Heinemann Ltd
15 Queen Street, Mayfair, London W1X 8BE

LONDON MELBOURNE TORONTO
JOHANNESBURG AUCKLAND

First published in Great Britain 1964

Reprinted 1968, 1971

434 29069 6

Reproduced and Printed in Great Britain by
Redwood Press Limited
Trowbridge & London

FOREWORD

KAHLIL GIBRAN has said: "Translation is an art in itself; it is the re-creative process of transforming the magic of one language into the magic of another."

To approach the works of a recognized master of any language is to face a task that presents peculiar difficulties; when such works have been inscribed with a heavenly informed wisdom and power, the difficulties become well-nigh insuperable.

This volume of prose poems, now presented for the first time in English, was undertaken by the translator as a labour of sincere devotion and with an earnest conviction of the power and importance of the original Arabic writings of Gibran Kahlil Gibran.

This poet, native to Becharre, born of Lebanese parents fifty-one years ago, lived a strangely single and separate life, notwithstanding his multitude of contacts with people in every station of existence, from beggars to royalty. There was a sense, impossible to define clearly, in which he was always and forever alone as a few and only a few of the men who have

v

walked this planet have also been. And there now remains here a handful of those persons who recognized Gibran for what he was, one of the Titans of world history.

The richness of his inheritance from remote Phœnician-Chaldean forefathers, enhanced by a long line of brilliant and cultured men and women, had woven for the ancient spirit a fitting garment which he wore with dignity and beneficence. Every stroke of his pen, every sweep of his brush, was a gesture of informed power. He has not written a meaningless, hardly a superfluous line, and he has left a store of peculiar treasure on parchment and canvas.

To the very close of his life Gibran wrote fertilely in Arabic, notwithstanding his mastery of English which served to set his name, several years ago, as one of the six men writing the most notable English.

This recognition of his pre-eminence with the language of his adoption was a gratification to Gibran, who smiled and said: " I who am but a guest to his language must needs treat it with deference. I may not take the liberties which its own sons may take."

With what immeasurable meed of deference, then, must the translator approach the great adventure of translating Gibran into English. The profound scholarship as well as the boldness and nobility of spiritual vision and power presents a vast emprise. I do not hesitate to say that this will never be done as Gibran himself would have done it. There is a Gibran English even as there is a Gibran Arabic, and both are definitely and subtly different from any other English and Arabic.

The present translation is an attempt to bring to the English-speaking world some of the earlier of this poet's Arabic prose poems, a form of which he was distinctly the originator in that ancient tongue. He has created a school of writing which has caught the vivid and sensitive imagination of the poetic and scholarly East, and of which he is recognized as father throughout the great Arabic-speaking race of three hundred million people.

This translation has been rendered with earnestness and devotion by a young countryman of Gibran's, a disciple who has felt in the original the appeal of a poignant mysticism and who has sedulously sought to invest the English version with the rare beauty of its Arabic prototype. To his efforts has been added the touch of an American writer who has spent years with Gibran English—one who has many times heard the poet himself speak these very poems, giving to them, in his translation, the fullness of his free, flowing English.

Perhaps some small measure of the heat from that deep fire of which the original poems were the flame may be felt herein; perhaps some rushlight of the poet's profound realization—the tragic beauty and rightness of life, and the supreme assurance that " We have eternity "—

may be found and followed; perhaps there may beat through the succeeding rhythms some echo of the poet's own heart-beat. That these things may be so is the hope of Andrew Ghareeb and myself.

And if they be so, then the work has been good work, and not a vain gesture to be lost in a world of futile gesturing.

BARBARA YOUNG

CONTENTS

Foreword   v

AT THE DOOR OF THE TEMPLE   3

REVELATION   12

THE SOUL   16

SONG OF THE NIGHT   19

MY SOUL COUNSELLED ME   21

MY BIRTHDAY   29

BE STILL, MY HEART   43

NIGHT   55

IN THE CITY OF THE DEAD   63

THE POET   69

FAME   75

EARTH   76

AT THE DOOR OF
THE TEMPLE

I purified my lips with the sacred fire to
    speak of love,
But when I opened my lips I found myself
    speechless.
Before I knew love, I was wont to chant
    the songs of love,
But when I learned to know, the words
    in my mouth became naught save
    breath,
And the tunes within my breast fell into
    deep silence.
In the past, when you would question me
    concerning the secrets and the mys-
    teries of love,
I would speak and answer you with assur-
    ance.
But now that love has adorned me with
    vestments,

I come, in my turn, to question you of all
the ways of love, and all its wonders.
Who among you can answer me?
I come to question you about my self and
that which is in me.
Who among you can reveal my heart to my
heart,
And disclose my self to my self?
Tell me now, what flame is this that burns
within my bosom,
Consuming my strength, and melting my
hopes and my desires?
What hands are these, light, gentle, and
alluring,
Which enfold my spirit in its hours of
loneliness
And pour into the vessel of my heart a
wine mixed of the bitterness of joy
And the sweetness of pain?
What wings are these beating around my
bed in the long silence of the night,
So that I am wakeful, watching — I know
not what;
Listening to that I do not hear, and gazing
upon that I do not see;

Meditating on that I do not comprehend,
and possessing that I have not at-
tained.

Ay, wakeful am I, sighing,

For to me sighs and griefs are lovelier than
the ring of joy and laughter;

Wakeful am I in the hand of an unseen
power that slays me and then quick-
ens me,

Even until the day dawns and fills the
corners of my house with light.

Then do I sleep, while between my with-
ered eyelids the shadows of my wake-
fulness still quiver,

And above my bed of stone hovers the
figure of a dream.

>>>>>>>

And what is this that we call love?

Tell me, what is this mystic secret hid-
ing behind the semblance of our
life,

And living in the heart of our existence?

What is this vast release coming as a cause
to all effects, and as an effect unto all
causes?

What is this quickening that gathers death
    and life and from them creates a
    dream
More strange than life, and deeper far
    than death?
Tell me, my brothers, tell me, which of
    you would not awake from this sleep
    of life
When your spirit feels the touch of love's
    white fingers?
Which of you would not forsake his father
    and his mother and his birthplace
When the maiden his heart loves calls out
    to him?
Which of you would not cross the desert
    and climb the mountain and sail the
    seas
To seek her to whom your spirit yearns?
What youth, indeed, would not follow to
    the earth's uttermost bounds,
If one awaits him there whose breath and
    voice and touch he shall find sweet
    and wholesome?
What man would not thus burn his soul
    as incense

Before a god who regards his craving and
　　grants him his petition?

　　　　　　≫≫≫≫≫

It was but yesterday that I stood at the
　　door of the temple
Questioning the passers-by concerning
　　the mysteries and the benefits of
　　love.
And a man passed by, of middle age,
　　wasted and with a scowling counte-
　　nance, and he said:
" Love is an inborn weakness which we
　　have inherited from the first man."
Then a youth, strong and stalwart of body
　　and arm, came chanting:
" Love is a resolution which accompanies
　　our being, and binds this present
　　with the ages past and future."
And now a sad-faced woman, passing,
　　sighed and said:
" Love is a deadly venom which dark and
　　fearful vipers diffuse in space from
　　the abyss of hell,
So that it descends in dew upon the thirsty
　　soul,

And the soul therefrom becomes for a mo-
ment drunken, then sobered for a
year, and dead an æon."
But a young maiden, rosy, and with laugh-
ing lips, said:
" See, love is a nectar which the brides of
dawn pour for the strong
So that they rise glorified before the stars
of night, and joyous before the sun
of day."
Thereafter came a man in a garment of
sombre black, and a loose beard that
fell upon his breast, and he said
sternly:
" Love is a stupidity which comes with the
dawn of youth and is gone with its
eventide."
And one followed him with face radiant
and serene, saying in tranquil joy:
" Love is a heavenly wisdom that lights
our inner and outer eye
So that we may behold all things even as
the gods."
Then passed by a blind man questioning
the ground with his old staff, and

there was a wailing in his voice as he said:

" Love is a dense fog to enshroud the soul, and veil from it the shows of life,

So that the soul sees naught but the shadows of its desires

Lost among rocky steeps,

And hears naught but the echo of its voice shouting from the valleys of desolation."

Then passed by a young man playing upon a lyre and singing:

" Love is a celestial light shining from the innermost of the sensitive self to illumine all about it,

That it may behold the worlds as a procession moving in green meadows,

And life as a dream of beauty between awakening and awakening."

And after the young man followed one decrepit, and with dragging feet, trembling, and he said:

" Love is the repose of the sad body in the silent grave,

And it is the security of the soul in the
fastnesses of eternity."
Then came a young child whose years
were but five, and he ran and
shouted:
" Love is my father, and love is my mother,
And no one knows of love but my mother
and my father."

>>>>>>

And now the day was done and all the
people were passed by before the
temple,
And each and every one had spoken of
love,
And in each word he had revealed his own
longing and desire
And had disclosed the secret mysteries of
life.

When evening was fully come, and the
moving throng had gone their ways,
And all was hushed,
I heard a voice within the temple say-
ing:

" All life is twain, the one a frozen stream,
  the other a burning flame,
And the burning flame is love."

Thereupon I entered into the temple and
  bowed myself, kneeling in supplica-
  tion
And chanting a prayer in my secret heart:
" Make me, O Lord, food for the burning
  flame,
And make me, O God, fuel for the sacred
  fire.
Amen."

REVELATION

When the night waxed deep and slumber
    cast its cloak upon the face of the
    earth,
I left my bed and sought the sea, saying
    to myself:
" The sea never sleeps, and the wakeful-
    ness of the sea brings comfort to a
    sleepless soul."
When I reached the shore, the mist had
    already descended from the moun-
    tain tops
And covered the world as a veil adorns the
    face of a maiden.

There I stood gazing at the waves, listen-
    ing to their singing, and considering
    the power that lies behind them —
The power that travels with the storm,
    and rages with the volcano, that

smiles with smiling flowers and makes melody with murmuring brooks.

After a while I turned, and lo,
I beheld three figures sitting upon a rock near by,
And I saw that the mist veiled them, and yet it veiled them not.

Slowly I walked toward the rock whereon they sat, drawn by some power which I know not.
A few paces off I stood and gazed upon them, for there was magic in the place
Which crystallized my purpose and bestirred my fancy.
And at that moment one of the three arose, and with a voice that seemed to come from the sea depths he said:
" Life without love is like a tree without blossoms or fruit.
And love without beauty is like flowers without fragrance, and fruit without seeds.

Life, Love, and Beauty are three entities
   in one self, free and boundless,
Which know neither change nor separa-
   tion."
This he said, and sat again in his place.

Then the second figure arose, and with a
   voice like the roar of rushing waters
   he said:
" Life without rebellion is like the seasons
   without a spring.
And rebellion without right is like spring
   in an arid and barren desert.
Life, Rebellion, and Right are three enti-
   ties in one self,
And in them is neither change nor separa-
   tion."
This he said, and sat again in his place.

Then the third figure arose, and spoke
   with a voice like the peal of the thun-
   der, saying:
" Life without freedom is like a body with-
   out a spirit.
And freedom without thought is like a
   spirit confounded.

Life, Freedom, and Thought are three en-
tities in one eternal self,
Which neither vanish nor pass away."

Then the three arose and with voices of
majesty and awe they spoke:
" Love and all that it begets,
Rebellion and all that it creates,
Freedom and all that it generates,
These three are aspects of God . . .
And God is the infinite mind of the finite
and conscious world."

Then silence followed, filled with the stir-
ring of invisible wings and the tremor
of the ethereal bodies.
And I closed my eyes, listening to the echo
of the saying which I heard.

When I opened my eyes, I beheld naught
but the sea hidden beneath a blanket
of mist;
And I moved closer toward that rock
And I beheld naught but a pillar of incense
rising unto the sky.

THE SOUL

. . . And the God of Gods created the
   soul, fashioning it for beauty

He gave unto it the gentleness of a breeze
   at dawn, the scent of flowers, the love-
   liness of moonlight.

He gave unto it also the cup of joy, and He
   said:

" You shall not drink of this cup save that
   you have forgotten the past and re-
   nounced the future."

He gave unto it also the cup of sorrow,
   saying:

" Drink that you may understand the
   meaning of joy."

Then God bestowed within the soul love
   that would depart with the first sigh
   of content,

And sweetness that would flee from the
   first word of arrogance.

He made a heavenly sign to guide it in the
    path of truth.

He placed in its depths an eye that would
    behold the unseen.

He created within it a fancy to flow like a
    river with phantoms and moving fig-
    ures.

He clothed it in garments of longing
    woven by angels, from the rainbow.

Within it He placed also the darkness of
    bewilderment, which is the shadow
    of light.

And God took fire from the forge of anger,

Wind blowing from the desert of igno-
    rance;

Sand He gathered from the seashore of
    selffulness

And dust from beneath the feet of the
    ages;

Thus He fashioned man.

And unto man He gave blind strength that
    leaps into a flame in moments of mad
    passion, and lies down before desire.

God gave him life which is the shadow of
    death.

And the God of Gods smiled and wept,
    and He knew a love which hath no
    bound nor end;
Thus He united man and his soul.

SONG OF THE NIGHT

The night is hushed,
And the dreams hide in silence.
The moon is rising —
She has eyes to watch the day.

Come, daughter of the fields,
And let us go
Into the vineyards
Where the lovers meet.
For it may be
That there we, too, may quench
With love's good vintage
The drouth of our desire.

Hearken, the nightingale
Pours forth his song
Into the valleys
Which the hills have filled
With the green scent of mint.

Fear not, beloved,
The stars will keep the secret of our meet-
     ing,
And the soft mist of night
Veil our embrace.

Fear not —
The young bride of the djinns
In her enchanted cave
Lies sleeping, drunk with love,
And well-nigh hidden
From the houri's eyes.

And even should the king of the djinns
     pass by,
Then love will turn him back.
For is he not a lover as I am,
And shall he disclose
That which his own heart suffers?

MY SOUL COUNSELLED
ME

My soul spoke unto me and counselled me
    to love all that others hate,
And to befriend those whom others de-
    fame.
My soul counselled me and revealed unto
    me that love dignifies not alone the
    one who loves, but also the beloved.
Unto that day love was for me a thread of
    cobweb between two flowers, close
    to one another;
But now it has become a halo with neither
    beginning nor end,
Encircling all that has been, and waxing
    eternally to embrace all that shall be.

>>>>>>

My soul counselled me and taught me to
    see beauty veiled by form and colour.

My soul charged me to gaze steadfastly
upon all that is deemed ugly until it
appears lovely.

Before my soul had thus charged and
counselled me,

I had seemed to see beauty like unto wa-
vering torches between pillars of
smoke;

But now the smoke has dispersed and
vanished and I see naught but the
burning.

❧❧❧❧❧❧

My soul counselled me and charged me to
listen for voices that rise neither from
the tongue nor the throat.

Before that day I heard but dully, and
naught save clamour and loud cries
came to my ears;

But now I have learned to listen to silence,

To hear its choirs singing the songs of ages,

Chanting the hymns of space, and disclos-
ing the secrets of eternity.

❧❧❧❧❧❧

My soul spoke unto me and counselled me
to quench my thirst with that wine

which may not be poured into
cups,
Nor lifted by hands, nor touched by lips.
Unto that day my thirst was like a dim
spark laid in ashes
To be put out by a draught from any
spring;
But now my strong yearning has become
my cup,
Love has become my wine, and loneliness
my joy.

>>>>>>

My soul counselled me and charged me to
seek that which is unseen;
And my soul revealed unto me that the
thing we grasp is the thing we desire.
In other days I was content with warmth
in winter, and with a cooling zephyr
in the summer season;
But now my fingers are become as mist,
Letting fall all that they have held, to min-
gle with the unseen that I now desire.

>>>>>>

My soul spoke to me and invited me to
breathe the fragrance from a plant

That has neither root nor stalk nor blos-
  som, and that no eye has seen.
Before my soul counselled me thus, I
  sought perfumes in the gardens,
In jars of sweet-smelling herbs and vessels
  of incense;
But now I am aware only of an incense
  that may not be burned,
I breathe an air more fragrant than all
  earth's gardens and all the winds of
  space.

My soul counselled me and charged me to
  answer and say: " I follow," when
  the unknown and the adventurous
  call unto me.
Hitherto I had answered naught but the
  voice of the crier in the market-place,
Nor did I pursue aught save roads charted
  and well trodden;
But now the known has become a steed
  that I mount to seek the unknown,
And the road has become a ladder by
  which I may climb to the perilous
  summit.

My soul counselled me and admonished
    me to measure time with this saying:
" There was a yesterday and there shall
    be a tomorrow."
Unto that hour I deemed the past an epoch
    that is lost and shall be forgotten,
And the future I deemed an era that I may
    not attain;
But now I have learned this:
That in the brief present all time, with all
    that is in time,
Is achieved and come true.

⇒⇒⇒⇒⇒

My soul spoke and revealed unto me that
    I am not bound in space by the
    words:
" Here, there, and over there."
Hitherto I stood upon my hill, and every
    other hill seemed distant and far
    away;
But now I know that the hill whereon I
    dwell is indeed all hills,
And the valley whereunto I descend com-
    prehends all valleys.

My soul counselled me and besought me
    to watch while others sleep
And to seek my pillow while they are
    wakeful,
For in all my years I had not perceived
    their dreams, nor they mine.
But now I am winged by day in my dream-
    ing,
And when they sleep I behold them free
    upon the night,
And I rejoice in their freedom.

>>>>>>

My soul counselled me and charged me
    lest I be exalted because of overpraise
And lest I be distressed for fear of blame.
Until that day I doubted the worth of my
    own handiwork;
But now I have learned this:
That the trees blossom in spring, and bear
    fruit in summer,
And drop their leaves in autumn to become
    utterly naked in winter
Without exaltation and without fear or
    shame.

My soul counselled me and assured me
That I am neither higher than the pygmy
    nor lower than the giant.
Before that day I beheld mankind as two
    men,
The one a weakling whom I derided or
    pitied,
And the other a mighty man whom I would
    either follow, or oppose in rebellion.
But now I know that I was formed even
    from the same dust of which all men
    are created,
That my elements are their elements, and
    my inner self is their inner self.
My struggle is their struggle, and their
    pilgrimage is mine own.
If they transgress, I am also the transgres-
    sor,
And if they do well, then I have a share in
    their well-doing.
If they arise, I too arise with them; if they
    stay behind, I also, to company them.

⋙⋙⋙

My soul counselled me and instructed me

to see that the light which I carry is
   not my light,
That my song was not created within me;
For though I travel with the light, I am
   not the light,
And though I am a lute fastened with
   strings,
I am not the lute-player.

~>>>>>>

My soul counselled me, my brother, and
   enlightened me.
And oftentimes has your soul counselled
   and enlightened you.
For you are like me, and there is no dif-
   ference between us
Save that I speak of what is within me in
   words that I have heard in my silence,
And you guard what is within you, and
   your guardianship is as goodly as my
   much speaking.

MY BIRTHDAY

(Written while studying art in Paris, January 6, 1908)

On the day my mother gave me birth,
On that day five-and-twenty years ago,
Silence placed me in the vast hands of life,
    abounding with struggle and conflict.
Lo, five-and-twenty times have I jour-
    neyed round the sun.
How many times the moon has journeyed
    round me I do not know.
But this I know, that I have not yet
    learned the secrets of light,
Nor have I understood the mysteries of
    darkness.

Five-and-twenty times have I journeyed
    with the earth, the moon, the sun and
    stars encircling the universe.
Lo, now my soul whispers the names of
    cosmic systems

Even as the caverns of the sea resound to
the waves,
For the soul exists, a current in the cos-
mos, but does not know its power.
And the soul chants the cosmic rhythm,
high and low,
Yet attains not the fullness of its har-
monies.

Five-and-twenty years ago Time wrote me
down in the book of this strange and
awful life.
Lo, a word am I, signifying now nothing
and now many things.
On that day of every year what thoughts
and what memories throng my
soul!
They halt before me — the procession of
the days gone by,
The parade of the phantoms of the
night —
Then are they swept away, even as the
wind sweeps clouds from the hori-
zon;
They vanish in the darkness of my house

as the songs of the rivulets in deso-
late and distant valleys.

On that day, every year, those spirits
    which have shaped my spirit
Come seeking me from the far ends of the
    worlds,
And chanting words of sorrowful remem-
    brance.
Then they are gone, to hide behind the
    semblance of this life,
Even as birds descending to a threshing-
    floor and finding no seeds to feast
    upon,
Hover but a moment and fly hence to seek
    another place.

Ever upon that day the meanings of my
    past life stand before me, like dim
    mirrors
Wherein I look for a while and see naught
    but the pallid corpse-like faces of the
    years,
Naught but the wrinkled and aged visages
    of hopes and dreams long lost.

Once more I look upon those mirrors, and
there behold only my own still face.
I gaze thereon beholding naught but sad-
ness.
I question sadness and I find it has no
speech;
Yet could sadness speak, methinks it
would utter a sweeter word than joy.

For five-and-twenty years I have loved
much,
And oftentimes have I loved what others
hate.
Yet what I loved as a child I love now,
And what I now love I shall love unto the
end of life;
For love is all I have, and none shall make
me lose it.

Oftentimes have I loved death,
Called death sweet names and spoken of
it in loving words both openly and
secretly.
Yet though I have not forgotten, nor
broken the vows of death,

I have learned to love life also.

For death and life have become equal to
me in beauty and in joy;

They have shared in the growth of my
yearning and desire,

And they have divided my love and ten-
derness.

Freedom also have I loved, even as life and
death.

And as my love grew, so grew also my
knowledge of men's slavery to tyr-
anny and contempt,

The while I beheld their submission to
idols hewn by the dark ages,

Reared in ignorance and polished by the
lips of slaves.

But I loved these slaves as I loved free-
dom, and I pitied them, for they are
blind men

Kissing the jaws of foul bloodthirsty
beasts, and seeing not;

Sucking the venom of malignant vipers,
and feeling not;

Digging their graves with their own hands,
and knowing not.

Freedom have I loved more than aught
else,

For I have found freedom like unto a
maiden wasted from privation and
seclusion

Till she became a ghost that moves
among the houses in the lonely
streets,

And when she calls out to the passers-by,
they neither hear nor look.

Like all men, during these five-and-twenty
years I have loved happiness;

I have learned to awake at every dawn and
seek it, even as they.

But never have I found it in their ways,

Nor seen the trace of the footsteps of hap-
piness on the sand near their man-
sions,

Nor have I heard the echo of its voice from
the windows of their temples.

I sought alone to find it.

I heard my soul whisper in my ear:

" Happiness is a maiden born and reared
in the fastness of the heart;
She comes never from beyond its walls."
Yet when I opened the portal of my heart
to find happiness,
I saw therein her mirror and her bed and
her garments, but herself I could not
find.

Mankind have I loved. Ay, much have I
loved men,
And men in my opinion are three:
The one who curses life, the one who
blesses it, and the one who contem-
plates it.
The first I have loved for his misery, the
second for his beneficence, and the
third for his wisdom.

>>>>>>

Thus passed the five-and-twenty years,
And thus my days and nights, pursuing
each other down my life
As the leaves of trees scatter before the
winds of autumn.
And today I pause remembering, even as

35

a weary climber half-way to the sum-
mit,
And I look backward, and to right and
left, but I see no treasure any-
where
Which I may claim and say: " This is
mine own."

Nor do I find in the seasons of my years
any harvest
Save only sheets of fair white paper traced
over with markings of black ink,
And strange and fragmentary canvases
filled in with lines and colours, both
harmonious and inharmonious.
In these have I shrouded and buried the
loveliness and the freedom that I
have thought and dreamed,
Even as the ploughman who goes to the
field to sow his seeds in furrows
Returns to his house at eventide hoping
and waiting.
But I, though I have sowed well the seeds
of my heart,
Yet I have neither hoped nor waited.

And now that I have reached this season
  of my life,
The past seems hidden behind a mist of
  sighs and grief,
And the future revealed through the veil
  of the past.

I pause and gaze at life from my small
  window;
I behold the faces of men, and I hear their
  shouting rise into the sky.
I heed their footsteps falling among the
  streets of houses,
And I perceive the communion of their
  spirits, the eagerness of their desires,
  the yearning of their hearts.
I pause and behold the children throwing
  dust upon each other with laughter
  and loud cries.
I behold boys with their faces upward
  lifted as though they were reading
  an ode to youth written upon the
  margins of a cloud
Lined with the gleaming radiance of the
  sun.

I behold young maidens swaying to and
    fro, like branches of a tree,
Smiling like flowers, and gazing at the
    youths from behind eyelids
Quivering with love and soft desire.
I behold the aged walking slowly, with
    their low-bent backs,
Leaning upon their staffs and gazing fix-
    edly at the earth
As if their old dim eyes were searching in
    the dust for lost bright jewels.
I pause beside my window and I gaze at
    all these shapes and shadows
Moving and creeping silently about the
    city.

Then I look afar beyond the city to the
    wilderness,
And I behold all that is therein of dreadful
    beauty and of calling silence,
Its lofty mounds and little valleys, its
    springing trees and tremulous
    grasses,
Its flowers with perfume laden, and its
    whispering rivers,

Its wild birds singing, and all its humming
     wingèd life.

I gaze beyond the wilderness, and there,
     behold, the ocean —
With its deep wonders and mysterious se-
     crets, its hid treasures;
There I behold all that is upon the face of
     the raging, rushing, foaming waters,
And the spray that rises and the vapours
     that descend.

I peer far beyond the ocean and behold
     the infinity of space,
The drifting worlds, the glimmering con-
     stellations, the suns and moons, the
     fixed and the shooting stars;
And I behold the evidence of forces for-
     ever attracting and repelling, the
     wars of elements, creating, changing,
     and withal held prisoned within a law
     of no beginning and no end.

These things I contemplate through my
     small window, and I forget my five-
     and-twenty years,

And all the centuries which have preceded
    them,
And all the ages that shall follow.
Then my life, with its revelations and its
    mysteries, seems to me like the sigh-
    ing of a child
That trembles in the void of the eternal
    depths and heights.
Yet this atom, this self that I call *I*, makes
    ever a stirring and a clamour,
Lifting its wings toward the vast firma-
    ment,
Reaching its hands toward the four cor-
    ners of the earth,
Its being poised upon the point of time
    which gave it conscious life.

Then from the holy of holies where this
    living spark abides, a voice arises
    crying:
" Peace be with you, life!
Peace be with you, awakening!
Peace be with you, realization!
Peace be with you, day, whose abundant
    light enfolds the darkness of earth!

Peace be with you, night, whose darkness
reveals the light of heaven!
Peace be with you, seasons!
Peace be with you, spring, that renews the
youth of the earth!
Peace be with you, summer, that enriches
the glory of the sun!
Peace be with you, autumn, that bestows
the fruits of labour and the harvest
of toil!
Peace be with you, winter, that restores
with tempests the wasted strength of
nature!
Peace be with you, years, which disclose
what the years have hidden!
Peace be with you, ages, which restore
what the centuries have destroyed!
Peace be with you, time, which moves
with us unto the perfect day!
Peace be with you, spirit, that guards with
prudence the reins of life, hidden
from us by the sun!
Peace be with you, heart, that you are
moved to acclaim peace
The while you bathe in tears!

Peace be with you, lips, that you utter
    peace
The while you taste the bread of bitter-
    ness! "

BE STILL, MY HEART

Be still, my heart. Space does not hear
   you.
Be still, my heart. The ether, heavy with
   mourning and with lamentation, will
   not bear your songs.
Be still, for the phantoms of night will
   not heed the whisper of your mys-
   teries,
And the procession of darkness will not
   halt before your dreams.
Be still, my heart, be still until dawn.
For whoso waits the morning patiently
   will greet the morning with strength,
And whoso loves the light, by light shall he
   be loved.
Be still, my heart, and listen to my words.

In dreams I heard a blackbird singing
   above the mouth of a raging volcano,

And saw a lily lifting its head above the
    snow;
I saw a naked houri dancing among tomb-
    stones,
And a babe laughing the while it played
    with skulls.
All this I saw in a dream.

When I waked and looked about me, lo,
    I saw the volcano pouring forth its
    fury,
But I could not hear the blackbird singing.
I saw the heavens scattering snow over the
    hills and valleys,
Garmenting with its white shroud the si-
    lent lilies.
I saw the graves, row upon row, standing
    before the tranquillity of ages, but
    none amongst them dancing or pray-
    ing.

Then I beheld hills of skulls, but no
    laughter was there save the laughing
    wind.
Waking I saw naught but grief and sor-
    row.

Where, then, have the joys of dreams de-
    parted?
Where hides the splendour of our sleep,
And how has its image vanished?
How can the soul bear patiently until the
    shadow of its yearning shall return
    with sleep?

~~~~~~

Be still, my heart, and attend unto my
    words.
It was but yesterday that my soul was a
    tree, old and strong,
Whose roots penetrated to the depths of
    the earth and whose branches
    reached toward the infinite, bloom-
    ing in spring and bearing fruit in
    summer.
When autumn was come, I gathered the
    fruit on trays of silver and placed
    them at the cross-roads,
And the passers-by reached for the fruit
    and ate of it and walked their way.

When autumn was passed and its song was
    turned to wailing and a dirge,

I looked upon my trays and saw that men
   had left there but a single fruit;
And when I tasted, I found it bitter as
   aloes and sour as a green grape.
Then I said to myself:
" Woe unto me, for I have placed a curse
   upon the lips of men, and hostility in
   their bowels.
What then, my soul, have you done with
   the sweetness that your roots had
   sucked from the bosom of earth,
And with fragrance that your boughs had
   drunk from the light of the sun? "

Thereupon I uprooted the old and strong
   tree of my soul.
I severed it from its past and dismantled
   it of the memories of a thousand
   springs and a thousand autumns.

And I planted the tree of my soul in an-
   other place.
I set it in a field far from the roads of time,
   and I passed the night in wakefulness
   beside it, giving it to drink of my
   tears and my blood, and saying:

" There is a savour in blood, and a sweet-
ness in tears."

When spring returned, the tree of my soul
bloomed again, and bore fruit in the
summer season.
And when the autumn was come, I gath-
ered the ripe fruit once more, and I
placed it upon trays of gold at the
meeting-place of the roads.
And men passed by, but no one reached to
take of the fruit.
Then I took and ate, and I found the fruit
as sweet as honey, as luscious as nec-
tar, perfumed as the breath of jas-
mine, and mellow as the wine of
Babylon.
And I cried aloud, saying:
" Men do not desire blessedness upon
their lips, nor truth in their
bowels;
For blessedness is the daughter of tears,
and truth is but the son of pain."
Then I returned and sat down under the
shade of the lonely tree of my soul,

and in the field far from the roads of
time.

꿈꿈꿈꿈

Be still, my heart, be still until dawn.
Be still, for space is heavy with the odour
of dead things and cannot inhale
your living breath.
Be still, my heart, and listen to my voice.
It was but yesterday that my thought was
like a ship, rocked upon the waves of
the sea, and moving with the winds
from shore to shore.
And the ship of my thought was empty
save only for seven phials filled to the
brim with seven colours, even the
seven colours of the rainbow.

There came a time when I grew weary of
drifting upon the face of the waters,
and I said:
" I will return with the empty ship of my
thought to the harbour of the town
where I was born."
And as I sailed, I began to paint the sides
of my ship with the seven colours;

And it shone yellow as the sunset, azure
like the sky, and red as a blood-red
anemone;
And upon its sails and rudder I traced
sketches to allure and delight the eye.
And when it was done, the ship of my
thought appeared like the vision of a
prophet
Floating betwixt the two infinities, the sea
and the sky.

Now, when my ship reached port, behold,
all the people came to meet me;
With shout and joy they welcomed me and
they took me into the city,
Beating their tambourines and blowing
upon their reed flutes.
All this they did because my ship ap-
peared enchanting to their eyes;
But none boarded the ship of my thought,
Nor did any perceive that I had brought
my ship empty into port.

Then I said to myself:
" I have misled the people, and with seven

phials of colours have I deceived their inner and their outer eye."

And when a year was passed, again I boarded the ship of my thought and put out to sea.

I sailed to the isles of the East, and there I gathered myrrh and frankincense and sandalwood and brought them to my ship.

I sailed to the isles of the South, and from thence I brought gold, jade, and emerald, and every precious stone;

To the isles of the North I sailed, and found rare silks and velvets and broideries of every kind;

Thence to the isles of the West and got me coats of mail, and spears and swords, and divers weapons.

Thus I filled the ship of my thought with the costly and strange things of the earth,

And I turned back to the harbour of my own city, saying in my heart:

" Now shall my people praise me as a man
worthy of praise.
And now shall they indeed lead me into
the market-place with singing and
piping."

But, behold, when I reached the port, no
man came to meet and welcome me.
Alone I entered the streets of my city, but
no man looked upon me.
Even in the market-squares I stood, tell-
ing of all that I had brought of the
earth's fruit and goodly things.
But the people looked upon me with
laughter on their faces, and derision
on their lips.
And they turned from me.
Thus was I troubled and cast down, and I
turned me to the harbour.

No sooner did my eyes fall upon my ship
than I became aware of a certain
thing to which, in my voyaging and
seeking for good cargoes, I had paid
no heed;

E

So I cried out in humiliation:
" Behold, the waves of the sea have
washed the seven colours from my
ship
And now it appears but as a skeleton of
bones.
And the winds and the storms and the heat
of the sun have effaced from the sails
the images of wonder and delight,
And they seem now but as a faded and tat-
tered garment.
Truly I have gathered the earth's costly
treasures in a casket floating upon
the surface of the waters,
And returned unto my people, but they
turn from me,
For their eyes see naught but outward
show."

At that very moment I abandoned the
ship of my thought and sought the
city of the dead,
Where I sat amid the whitened graves and
pondered their secrets.

Be still, my heart. Be still until dawn.
Be still, though the tempest mock the
    whispering of your depths.
Be still, my heart, until dawn.
For whoso awaits the morning patiently,
The morning shall embrace him tenderly.

Behold, my heart, the dawn is come;
Speak, then, if you have yet the power of
    words.
Behold, my heart, the procession of the
    morning.
Did not the silence of the night stir in your
    depths a song wherewith to greet the
    morn?

Behold, the flight of doves and blackbirds
    above the valley;
Did not the awe of night strengthen your
    wings to fly with them?
Behold, the shepherds leading their flocks
    from the folds.
Did not the shadows of night urge your
    desire to follow also into the green
    meadows?

Behold, the young men and the maidens
hastening toward the vineyard.
Would you not rise and join them?

Arise, my heart. Arise and move with the
dawn.
For night is passed and the fears of night
have vanished with their black
dreams.
Arise, my heart, and lift your voice in
song;
For he who joins not the dawn with his
singing is but a child of darkness.

NIGHT

O Night, abiding-place of poets and of
    lovers and of singers,
O Night, where shadows dwell with spirits
    and with visions,
O Night, enfolder of our longing, our de-
    sire, our memory,
Vast giant standing betwixt the dwarfed
    evening clouds and the brides of
    dawn,
Girt with the sword of awe, crowned with
    the moon, and garmented with si-
    lence;
Who gazes with a thousand eyes into the
    depths of life,
And listens with a thousand ears to the
    sighs of desolation and of death!

↭↭↭↭↭

It is your darkness that reveals to us the
    light of heaven,

For the light of day has enshrouded us with the darkness of earth.

It is your promise that opens our eyes to eternity,

For the vanity of day had held us like blind men in the world of time and space.

It is your tranquil silence that unveils the secret of ever wakeful, ever restless spirits;

For day is a turbulent clamour wherein souls lie beneath the sharp hooves of ambition and desire.

O Night, you are a shepherd who gathers unto the fold of sleep the dreams of the weak and the hopes of the strong.

You are a seer who closes with his mystic fingers the eyelids of the wretched and lifts their hearts to a world more kindly than this world.

In the folds of your grey garments lovers have found their bower,

And upon your feet, wet with the dew of heaven, have the lonely-hearted wept their tears;

In the palms of your hands, fragrant with
the scent of field and vineyard, stran-
gers have laid down their longing and
despair;
To lovers you are a friend; to the lonely, a
comforter; to the desolate, a host.
In your deep shade the poet's fancies stir;
on your bosom the prophetic heart
awakes; upon your brow imagination
writes.
For to the poet you are a sovereign, to the
prophet a vision, and to the thinker
an intimate.

～～～～～

When my soul became weary of man, and
my eyes were tired of gazing upon
the face of the day,
I sought the distant fields where the shad-
ows of bygone ages sleep.
There I stood before a dark and silent be-
ing moving with a thousand feet over
the mountain, and over the valley
and the plain.
There I gazed into the eyes of darkness

and listened to the murmuring of in-
visible wings.
There I felt the touch of formless gar-
ments and was shaken by the terrors
of the unseen.

There I saw you, Night, tragic and beau-
tiful and awesome,
Standing between the heaven and the
earth, with clouds for your garment,
girdled with the fog,
Laughing at the light of the sun and mock-
ing the supremacy of the day,
Deriding the multitude of slaves who
kneel sleepless before their idols,
and contemptuous of kings who lie
asleep and dreaming in their beds of
silk,
There I beheld you gazing into the eyes of
thieves, and I beheld you keeping
guard above the babe in slumber;
I saw you weeping before the smiles of
prostitutes, and smiling at the tears
of lovers,
And lifting with your right hand the great-

hearted, and with your feet tramp-
ling the mean-spirited.

There I saw you, Night, and you saw me;
You, in your awful beauty, were to me a
father, and I, in my dreams, was a
son;
For the curtains of being were drawn
away, and the veil of doubt was rent;
You revealed your secret purposes unto
me, and I told you all my hopes and
my desires.
Then was your majesty turned into mel-
ody more beautiful than the gentle
whisper of flowers,
And my fears were transformed into trust
more than the trust of birds;
And you lifted me and placed me on your
shoulders,
And you taught my eyes to see, my ears to
hear, my lips to speak, and my heart
to love;
With your magic fingers you touched my
thought,
And my thought poured forth like a flow-

ing, singing stream, bearing away all
that was withered grass.
And with your lips you kissed my spirit,
and it kindled into flames
Devouring every dead and dying thing.

❧❧❧❧❧

I followed you, O Night, until I became
like unto you;
I went as your companion until your de-
sires became mine;
I loved you until my whole being was in-
deed a lesser image of your own.
For within my dark self are glowing stars
which passion scatters at evening and
doubt gathers at dawn;
And within my heart is a moon that strug-
gles, now with thick clouds, and now
with a procession of dreams that fills
all space.
Now within my awakened soul dwells a
peace that reveals the lover's secret
and the worshipper's prayer;
And upon my head rests a veil of mystery
which the agony of death may rend,

but the songs of youth shall weave
again.

I am like you, O Night, and if men shall
deem me boastful,
Do they not boast of their resemblance to
the day?
I am like you, and like you I am accused
of much that I am not.
I am like you with all my dreams and all
my hopes and being.
I am like you, even though dusk does not
crown me with its golden fleece.
I am like you, though morn does not adorn
my trailing raiment with pearl and
rose.
I am like you, though I am not yet belted
with the milky way.
I too am a night, vast and calm, yet fet-
tered and rebellious.
There is no beginning to my darkness and
no end to my depths.
When the souls of the departed rise to
pride themselves upon the light of
joy,

My night soul shall descend glorified by
the darkness of its sorrow.
I am like you, O Night, and when my
dawn comes, then also shall come my
end.

IN THE CITY OF THE DEAD

It was but yesterday I escaped the tumult
    of the city
And went forth to walk in the silent fields;
And I came unto a lofty hill
Where nature had bestowed the gifts of
    her bountiful hand.
I ascended the hill and looked back upon
    the city.
And lo, the city appeared, with all its tow-
    ers and temples,
To lie beneath a cloud of thick dark smoke
    that rose up from its forges and its
    factories.

As I sat contemplating from afar the
    works of man,
It seemed that most of them are vain and
    futile.

And heartily I turned my mind away from all that the sons of Adam have wrought,

And looked upon the fields, the seat of God's great glory.

And in their midst I beheld a graveyard with tombstones of fair marble, and with cypress trees.

There, between the city of the living and the city of the dead, I sat

And mused upon the endless struggle and the ceaseless turbulence in life,

And the enveloping silence and vast dignity in death.

On the one side I beheld hope and despair, love and hate, riches and poverty, belief and unbelief;

And on the other, dust in dust which nature intermingles,

Fashioning therefrom its world of green and growing things that thrive in the deep silence of the night.

While thus I pondered, behold, a great
crowd, marching slowly, caught my
vision,
And I heard music filling the air with
dreary tunes.
Before my eyes passed a procession of the
great and the lowly of mankind,
Walking together in procession at the fu-
neral of a man who had been rich and
powerful,
The dead followed by the living.
And these wept and cried aloud, filling
the day with their wailings and their
lamentations,
Even unto the burial-place.
And here the priests offered up prayers
and swung their censers,
And the pipers blew mournfully upon
their pipes.
The orators stood forth with sounding
words of eulogy,
And the poets, bemoaning with their
studied verses,
Until all had come unto a weary end.

And then the crowd dispersed, revealing a
proud tombstone which the stone-
cutters had vied in making,
And many wreaths of flowers, and gar-
lands woven by deft and skilful
fingers.
Then the procession returned toward the
city, while I sat watching from afar,
and musing.

And now the sun was sinking toward the
west, and the shadows of the rocks
and trees began to lengthen and dis-
card their raiment of light.
At that moment I looked, and lo, two men
bearing upon their shoulders a coffin
of plain wood;
And after them a woman came in ragged
garments,
A babe at her breast, and at her feet a dog
that looked now to the woman, now
to the wooden casket.
Only these, in the procession at the fu-
neral of a man who had been poor
and humble —

The wife whose silent tears bespoke her
      sorrow,
A baby crying because his mother wept,
      and a faithful beast who would fol-
      low also in his dumb grief.
And when these reached the place of
      graves,
They lowered the coffin down into a pit in
      the far corner, well removed from the
      lofty marble tombs.
Then they turned back in silence and in
      desolation,
And the dog's eyes looked oftentimes to-
      ward the last dwelling-place of his
      friend and master,
Until they had disappeared from sight
      behind the trees.

Thereupon I bent my eyes first upon the
      city of the living, and said to myself:
" This is for the rich and powerful men ";
Then I looked upon the city of the dead,
      saying:
" And this is for the rich and powerful
      men."

And I cried aloud: " Where, then, is the
  abiding-place of those who are weak
  and poor, O Lord? "
This I said, and gazed up toward the
  heaven of clouds, glorious with the
  golden rays of the great sun.
And I heard a voice within me saying: " It
  is there! "

THE POET

An exile am I in this world.

An exile am I and alone, tormented by my
aloneness, which ever directs my
thought to a magic and unknown
realm

And fills my dreams with shadows of a
region distant and unseen.

An exile am I from my kinsmen and my
countrymen, and should I meet one
of them, I would say to myself:

" Who, then, is this one? Where is it I
have known him?

What bond unites me to him, and why do
I draw near to sit beside him? "

An exile am I from myself, and should I
hear my own tongue speak, my ear
finds the voice strange.

Sometimes I look within and behold my
   secret self, a hidden self that laughs
   and weeps, that dares and fears.
Then my being marvels at my being, and
   my spirit questions mine own spirit.
Yet I remain an exile, unknown, lost in the
   mist, clothed with the silence.

An exile am I from my body; and when I
   pause before a mirror, behold, in my
   face is that which my soul has not
   conceived, and in my eyes that which
   my depths do not contain.
When I walk upon the streets of the city,
   the children follow after me, shout-
   ing:
" Behold the blind man! Let us give him a
   staff to lean upon."
And in haste I flee from them.
If I meet a bevy of maidens, they cleave to
   my garments, singing:
" He is deaf as a rock! Let us fill his ears
   with harmonies of love and passion."
And from them I flee also.
Whenever I approach the middle-aged in

the market-place, they gather about me, crying:

" He is as mute as a tomb! Let us straighten his twisted tongue."

And I hasten from them in fear.

And if I pass by a company of elders, they point their trembling fingers toward me, saying:

" He is a madman who has lost his reason in the land of the Djinns and Ghouls! "

❧❧❧❧❧❧

An exile am I in this world.

An exile am I, for I have traversed the earth both East and West,

Yet I found not my birthplace, nor one who knew me or had heard my name.

In the morning I awake to find myself imprisoned in a darkened cavern

Where vipers threaten from above, and every crawling thing infests the walls and ground.

When I seek the outer light, the shadows of my body march ahead of me —

Whereto I know not, seeking that I do not

understand, grasping that for which
I have no need.

When eventide is come and I return and
lie upon my bed of thorn and feather,

Strange thoughts beguile me, both fear-
some and joyous, and desires be-
siege me with their pains and their
delights.

When it is midnight, the shades of bygone
ages fall upon me, and spirits of for-
gotten regions visit me and look upon
me,

And I gaze also upon them, and speak to
them and ask of ancient things,

And with kindliness and smiles they an-
swer me.

But when I would hold them and keep
them, they escape me

And fade as they were but smoke upon
the air.

❧❧❧❧❧

An exile am I in this world.

An exile am I, and no man understands
the language of my soul.

I pace the wilderness and I behold the

rivulets climbing from the depths of
the valley to the mountain top;
Before my eyes the naked trees come into
bloom and bear their fruit and scat-
ter their dead leaves, all in one mo-
ment.
And before my eyes their boughs fall to
the lowland and are turned into dark
serpents.

Ay, strange are my visions, like unto the
visions of no man,
For I see birds lifting their wings unto the
morning with songs, and then with
lamentation;
I see them alight and change before my
eyes into nude women with long,
loosened hair
Who gaze at me from behind eyelids
painted for love, and who smile upon
me with lips dipped in honey,
And who stretch white hands to me, per-
fumed with frankincense and myrrh.
And even as I gaze, they vanish like a
shaken mist,

Leaving in space the echo of their mock-
ing laughter.

❧❧❧❧❧

An exile am I in this world.
A poet am I who gathers in verse what life
scatters in prose;
And scatters in prose what life gathers in
verse.
And hence an exile am I, and an exile I
shall remain until death lifts me up
and bears me even unto my country.

FAME

I walked upon the sand at ebb-tide.
And bending down, I wrote a line upon the
   sand.
And in that line I wrote what my mind
   thought
And what my soul desired.

And when the tide was high,
I returned to that very shore,
And of that which I had written I found
   naught.
I found only the staff-marks of one who
   had walked blindly.

EARTH

With might and power earth springs forth
    out of earth;
Then earth moves over earth with dignity
    and pride;
And earth from earth builds palaces for
    kings,
And lofty towers and goodly temples for
    all people,
And weaves strange myths, strict laws,
    and subtle dogmas.

When all these things are done, earth
    wearies of earth's labour,
And from its light and darkness it creates
    grey shadows, and soft drowsy fan-
    cies, and enchanting dreams.
Earth's slumber then beguiles earth's
    heavy eyelids,
And they close upon all things in deep and
    quiet slumber.

And earth calls out unto earth, saying:
" Behold, a womb am I, and I am a tomb;
A womb and a tomb I shall remain forever,
Ay, even until the stars are no more,
And until the suns are turned into dead
ashes."